What Do We Know About Werewolves?

by Nico Medina

illustrated by Manuel Gutierrez

Penguin Workshop

This one goes out to Shakira, la loba más especial. "Arooo!"—NM

A Nazareno Cruz—MG

PENGUIN WORKSHOP
An imprint of Penguin Random House LLC
1745 Broadway, New York, NY 10019
penguinrandomhouse.com

Library of Congress Cataloging-in-Publication Data is available.

First published in the United States of America by Penguin Workshop, 2026

Manufactured in the United States of America
CJKW

ISBN 9798217141630 (paperback)
10 9 8 7 6 5 4 3 2 1

ISBN 9798217141647 (library binding)
10 9 8 7 6 5 4 3 2 1

The authorized representative in the EU for product safety and compliance is Penguin Random House Ireland, Morrison Chambers, 32 Nassau Street, Dublin D02 YH68, Ireland, https://eu-contact.penguin.ie.

Contents

What Do We Know About Werewolves?

Nineteen eighty-two was the first year that an Academy Award was given for makeup in a motion picture. The famous award, more commonly known as an Oscar, went to Rick Baker. He had created the special effects for a movie called *An American Werewolf in London*.

An American Werewolf in London

Moviegoers were both shocked and mesmerized by one particular scene in the film, in which the main character—a college student who is bitten by a wolf—transforms into a wolflike monster in a most horrific manner. He screams as his hands and feet lengthen painfully into paws. Thick hair sprouts from his skin as his face extends into a twisting, snarling snout. Sharp claws sprout from the man's fingertips. Audiences were wowed by how detailed the transformation was, and Rick Baker's special effects made some people almost believe that werewolves could be real.

Ever since the first humans left their shelters to hunt and gather food, wolves have fascinated us. When people began keeping livestock, wolves—always looking for an easy meal—became our enemies. We eventually hunted them nearly to extinction in Europe. And yet still,

we admired the wolf pack for what it was—a killer team, working together to survive—and, in some ways, we wanted to be like them.

Rick Baker had been making monsters all his life. The second mask that ten-year-old Rick made in 1960 was that of a Wolf Man, inspired by a classic movie. The special effects in 1941's *The Wolf Man* were not as advanced as those in *An American Werewolf in London*. But at the time, the on-screen man-to-wolf transformation was impressive—even scary!

Surely, though, audiences understood these frightening scenes weren't real. Werewolves and wolf men couldn't truly exist. Could they?

Tales about people becoming wolves have been told—and believed—for almost as long as people have been telling stories. From ancient Mesopotamia to the Americas, classical Greek mythology to the Twilight Saga of the twenty-first century.

In early human history, werewolf tales may have been created to help make sense of our world.

Today, we mostly tell them to give people a good scare at the movies.

CHAPTER 1
Early Werewolf Tales

Werewolves.

What comes to mind when you read that word?

Maybe it's what you've seen on TV and in the movies: Someone gets bitten by a wolf. Later, they begin to notice changes in their bodies, in their sense of smell and hearing. At the full moon, a terrifying transformation takes place. They become a violent werewolf possessing supernatural strength. The only thing that can stop them is a silver bullet—or the sunrise of a new day.

The world's earliest werewolf legends were quite different from all that.

In these tales, people were turned into

wolves by angry gods, or by wearing animal skins, not by wolf bites. In some myths, people would transform *themselves* into wolves—with or without a full moon in the sky. Werewolves were not always portrayed as mindless killers. Sometimes they were noble, helpful, or even heroic. And silver had no special effect on them.

In the *Epic of Gilgamesh*—the world's earliest known myth—Ishtar, the ancient Mesopotamian goddess of love and war, turns a shepherd who adores her into a wolf. The shepherd is then killed by his own dogs. This tale is as many as four thousand years old!

Sculpture of Ishtar

Still, many scholars consider the ancient Greek myth of King Lycaon of Arcadia to be the world's first werewolf legend. The name *Lycaon* gave us the word *lycanthropy* (say: lie-KANN-thro-pee)—the belief that one is a wolf or can become a wolf.

Lycaon was a mythological king. He lived only in legends. He was the son of Pelasgus, the first king of Arcadia. As the story goes, King Lycaon was hosting Zeus, the almighty king of the gods. But Lycaon doubted that Zeus was all-knowing. To prove it, Lycaon tried to trick Zeus into eating human flesh for dinner.

Zeus

King Lycaon

When Zeus realized that Lycaon was trying to deceive him, he burned down Lycaon's palace and transformed him into a wolf. "His clothes changed to coarse hair, his arms to legs. He was a wolf yet kept some human trace: the same gray hair, the same fierce face." This is how the first werewolf transformation was described by the poet Ovid (born 43 BCE).

Lycaon became thirsty for blood. He ran wildly among his flocks of sheep, his mouth foaming.

The myth came to be long before Ovid's time—before stories were even being written down. It was passed down through the ages by storytelling. Ovid's version of the legend is the most famous, but many others survive to this day. In one telling, Zeus turns Lycaon's fifty sons into wolves, too!

Lycaon's curse inspired a new ritual held by the people of Arcadia, a real place in Greece. According to the ancient Greek scholar Pliny the Elder (born c. 24 CE), this ritual to honor Zeus involved sacrificing one human alongside several animals atop Mount Lykaion (named for the mythical king). Their body parts were mixed together and then eaten by the people participating in the ritual.

Mount Lykaion

Whoever was unlucky enough to eat any of the human meat would instantly turn into a wolf! They would return to their human form only if they resisted eating people while in their wolf form . . . *for nine years*! The curse was a test of a person's humanity. If they passed, then they were considered good and could live once again as a human.

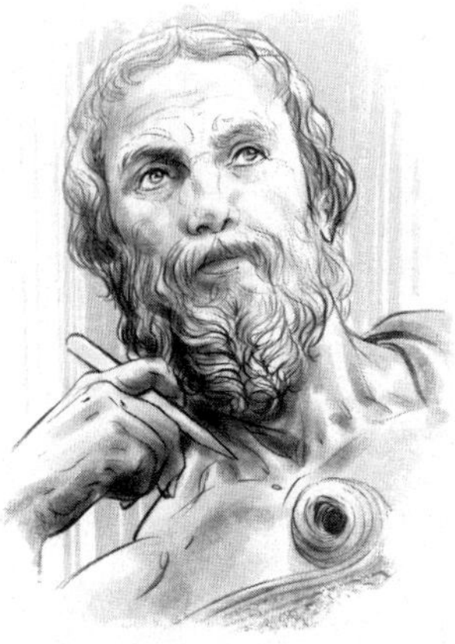

Herodotus

The Neuri, an ancient tribe from Eastern Europe, also had a wolf ritual. As told by the Greek historian Herodotus (born c. 485 BCE), for a few days every year, the Neurians used sorcery to transform themselves into wolves. While Herodotus said he didn't believe such tales, he did believe the Neurians were sorcerers with magical powers.

Another well-known werewolf story is the tale

of Niceros, a servant from ancient Rome who fell in love with a woman named Melissa. One night, Niceros decided to visit Melissa. He convinced a brave soldier to join him on his nighttime journey.

The two men set off under the bright moonlight. As they walked past a graveyard, something strange happened. Niceros's companion stopped, removed all his clothes, and urinated in a circle around the clothing like a dog marking its territory. Suddenly, the soldier transformed into a wolf and ran howling into the woods, and the pile of clothing turned to stone.

Terrified, Niceros continued on. When he reached Melissa's home, Melissa said she wished he'd arrived sooner, because a wolf had broken into their farm and slaughtered some livestock. The wolf would have killed every last animal had it not been for a servant stabbing its neck with a spear.

The next morning, Niceros saw a pool of blood where the pile of clothes had been the night before. When Niceros returned home, he saw the soldier lying in bed. A doctor was tending to a bloody wound on the man's neck. Niceros "saw at once that he was a fellow who could change his skin."

Clothing plays an important role in another werewolf story by a poet named Marie de France. Marie was born in France and lived in England from the late 1100s to the early 1200s. The story is about a nobleman named Bisclavret who also happens to be a werewolf. Each week,

Marie de France

he goes into the woods, hides his clothing in a secret spot, and transforms into a wolf. For three days, he hunts and feeds in the woods. To become human again, Bisclavret must return to his clothes.

When the nobleman's wife discovers his secret, she and another man conspire against him. While Bisclavret is in his wolf form, the other man steals his clothing, trapping Bisclavret in his wolf body.

One year later, Bisclavret meets the king in the woods. He's nearly killed by the king's hunting dogs, but when Bisclavret rushes to the king and kisses his feet, the king sees the humanity behind the wolf and spares his life. He brings Bisclavret back to live at court with him. Eventually, Bisclavret's wife reveals to the king where Bisclavret's clothing is hidden, and the curse is broken.

Wolves and werewolves also feature prominently in Norse mythology, the ancient belief of the Vikings of far northern Europe.

One of the Vikings' oldest werewolf tales is that of Sigmund and his son Sinfjötli (say: SIN-f'yote-lee). While prowling the woods for people and houses to rob, the two spotted a house that appeared to be empty. When they entered, they found two wealthy men sleeping soundly with wide gold rings on their fingers and two thick wolf skins hanging above them. Sigmund and his son stole the furry pelts.

After putting on the wolf skins, the father and son transformed into wolves. When they howled, they realized they could understand each other. The two walked deeper into the woods. They wanted to test their newfound wolf abilities, so they decided to separate and hunt for men. They agreed to howl for help if either wolf faced a group more than seven strong.

Sigmund was the first to encounter a group of men, and he howled for Sinfjötli. His son rushed to join him, and together they killed everyone. Then they separated again.

When Sinfjötli came upon a group of eleven men, he slew them all on his own. Afterward, he lay under an oak tree to rest. Sigmund arrived on the scene and demanded to know why Sinfjötli hadn't howled for help. The two argued, and Sigmund attacked his son, clawing at his throat.

Sigmund felt bad about injuring his son. He carried Sinfjötli into an underground den and looked after him while he recovered. After eleven days, the two were finally able to remove their wolf skins and transform back into humans. As soon as they did, they burned the enchanted pelts.

While most early werewolf legends are about men becoming wolves, there are some stories about women who are "she-wolves," too.

Signy

In one Norse legend, a woman named Signy was married to a cruel king. Her youngest brother had a sword from the god Odin that the king wanted. When Signy's brother refused to sell him the sword, the king decided to seek revenge. He lured Signy's ten brothers into the woods, ambushed them, and had them tied to a fallen tree.

For the next nine nights, a "huge and grimly" old she-wolf emerged at midnight to eat one of the brothers. On the tenth night, only Signy's youngest brother remained.

Signy sent a servant to her last surviving brother. She told him to smear honey on her brother's face and in his mouth. When the she-wolf came for her nightly meal, rather than attack Signy's brother, she licked the honey off his face. When she went for the last of the honey inside the boy's mouth, he bit down hard on her tongue. She thrashed about trying to free herself, breaking the boy loose from under the tree. The boy ripped out the she-wolf's tongue, killing her.

In many early legends, werewolves are portrayed in a negative light. But wolves were also respected for their strength, intelligence, and pack loyalty. The Vikings believed that when Odin created humans, he told them to take instruction from wolves: how to cooperate in the hunt, how to protect their families.

One brotherhood of Viking warriors known as the *Ulfhednar*, or "Wolf-skinners," looked to the wolf for strength in battle. They believed that Odin had granted them supernatural powers, including a resistance to pain, fire, and iron weapons. And they wore wolf pelts over their armor.

Before battle, the Wolf-skinners performed a ritual to connect with the spirit of the wolf. They might have consumed special herbs or teas that made them truly believe they had become wolves.

In battle, they fought ferociously, sometimes using their teeth and nails, howling wildly. They went *berserk*.

The Sea-Wolves

The Vikings were the most skilled navigators of their time. They sailed from their Scandinavian homelands to raid and conquer places, from Britain, Ireland, and France, all the way to Italy, North Africa, and Ukraine. They inspired such fear in the people they attacked that they were sometimes called "sea-wolves"—even "ware-wolves."

The Vikings were also ambitious tradesmen and explorers. Vikings from Sweden did business with merchants as far away as modern-day Turkey. Erik the Red established a Viking settlement in Greenland. And in the year 1000, Erik's son Leif Erikson became the first European to sail to North America.

This period, from 793 to 1066, is known as the Viking Age. The rise of Christianity in Europe eventually brought it to a close.

The Wolf-skinners were among the class of Viking warriors called the *Berserkir*, where the phrase *going berserk* comes from. Some *Berserkir* warriors dressed in bear or boar skins and embodied the spirits of those animals.

Viking Wolf-skinners were respected as brave warriors fighting for the glory of Odin. In tales like Marie de France's *Bisclavret*, werewolves could be noble and worthy of sympathy. In another early werewolf tale from Sweden, a peasant saves a band of weary travelers from starvation when he turns into a wolf and kills a sheep for them to eat. These positive images of wolves and werewolves were common throughout the Middle Ages (around 500–1450 CE).

Over time, portrayals of werewolves became more negative. As populations moved from the thickly wooded forests to the relative safety of villages and cities, the wilderness became a scarier and more dangerous place in people's minds.

Wolves—whose strength humans had respected for so many centuries—became associated with the devil. A thirteenth-century writer said wolves were "envious of mankind" and turned people's souls toward evil.

King Canute

King Canute, who ruled England from 1016 to 1035, warned against "the madly audacious werewolf"—to be careful that it not "bite too many of the spiritual flock." (This is the first time the word *werewolf* was ever recorded. It comes from *werewulf* in Old English, which means "man-wolf.") The "spiritual flock" were the people who practiced Christianity.

As the power of governments and religious institutions grew across Europe, the idea of werewolves and new stories about them became centered on their aggressive and hostile natures. They became seen as malevolent figures, born from witchcraft or possessed by demons. Werewolves were meant to be identified . . . and killed.

CHAPTER 2
Werewolf Trials

By the fifteenth century, Christianity had spread throughout Europe. But werewolf legends had been around since long before Jesus, and the Catholic Church was struggling to replace people's ancient traditions with their own.

The church declared that only God had the power to transform a person into something else, and that the devil could only create illusions to make a person *think* they had been transformed. By saying this, the church had taken the belief

in werewolves and turned it into something associated with evil and trickery.

The Roman Catholic Church was the most powerful Christian institution in Europe. But Protestantism, a new branch of Christianity, began to grow in the sixteenth century. Protestants and Catholics disagreed on many matters, so Protestants decided to establish their own church.

Each of these two groups of Christians wanted to strengthen their power and influence over the population. One way to do that was to root out evil by prosecuting and executing so-called werewolves. This would also serve as a warning to people about what would happen if they broke God's law.

Between the fifteenth and eighteenth centuries (the 1400s through the 1700s), thousands of people across Europe were put on trial by the church and by local governments for suspicion of werewolfery and witchcraft. In many cases, the accused were tortured until they confessed, so many might have lied just to survive.

Salem Witch Trials

Witch trials in Europe from the 1400s to the 1700s led to the execution of tens of thousands of people, most of them women. As the witch hysteria died down in Europe, it briefly took hold in British North America.

From 1692 to 1693, the village of Salem, Massachusetts, was the site of one of the most tragic events in American history. Eleven-year-old Abigail Williams and her nine-year-old cousin Betty were behaving strangely. They twisted their bodies in unnatural ways and spoke in odd, unknown languages. A doctor said they had been bewitched. The girls accused three townswomen of witchcraft, including Tituba, an enslaved Native American who worked in their house. The women were put on trial and found guilty.

Over the following months, more than two

hundred people were accused of witchcraft. Often, the courts didn't believe the accused when they proclaimed their innocence. Nineteen people were executed, and five died in prison. The village of Salem was gripped by witch hysteria until the courts finally declared they would hold no further trials. The Salem witch trials were the last such trials in the United States. They led to changes in the legal system to protect the accused.

Switzerland

The first time anyone was put on trial for werewolfery was in Switzerland. Beginning in 1428, hundreds of people in the Valais region were accused of witchcraft. Some of them had supposedly transformed into wolves and attacked people's cattle. Many were found guilty and sentenced to be burned alive.

In Besançon, France, in 1521, two shepherds named Pierre Burgot and Michel Verdun were put on trial for werewolfery and murder. Pope Leo X, head of the Catholic Church, sent representatives from the Vatican in Rome to oversee the trial. Pierre confessed that nineteen years earlier, he'd made a deal with the devil, who had appeared to him as a man dressed in black riding a black horse.

A storm had driven Pierre's flocks away, and Pierre feared they would never return and that he would starve. In exchange for helping him, Pierre agreed to serve the devil and to renounce God and his Christian faith. He sealed the deal with a kiss to the demon's cold black hand.

Years later, Pierre attended a midnight gathering of witches in the woods with Michel Verdun. Michel rubbed an ointment on Pierre that turned him into a wolf. Michel transformed, too, and they set off into the night and mauled a seven-year-old boy. Pierre and Michel also killed and ate people and livestock on several occasions. The two men were burned at the stake for their crimes.

Werewolves and witches were often blamed for anything from animal deaths and crop failure to drought and famine, and even unsolved murders. People who lived outside of mainstream society—including beggars, hermits, recent immigrants, and the mentally ill—were frequently accused of werewolfery or witchcraft because they were misunderstood.

In 1573, in St. Claude, France, Gilles Garnier, a poor immigrant living in the forest, was tried for the murder of several children. He was also accused of eating one of his victims on a Friday, when the church forbade eating meat.

Gilles confessed to these crimes but only after being tortured. The story he gave was very similar to Pierre Burgot's: Starving, he had made a pact with a demon and was given an ointment that turned him into a werewolf. But were these confessions false? Were they given only under the stress of being on trial?

St. Claude's grand judge, Henri Boguet, believed that a large group of witches and werewolves was menacing the area. In 1610, he published a book about sorcerers and werewolves—and how to judge them in court. Over his lifetime, Boguet sentenced *hundreds* of people to death for werewolfery and witchcraft. But there was little to no proof for the things Boguet claimed.

The 1589 case of Peter Stubbe in Bedburg, Germany, was one of the most infamous trials. The details of Peter's alleged crimes were so sensational, news of his trial reached as far as London.

Peter Stubbe admitted to practicing black magic since he was a boy, and his crimes took place over a period of twenty-five years. He said that the devil had given him a belt that turned him into a "greedy, devouring wolf . . .

with most sharp and cruel teeth, a huge body and mighty paws."

While in his wolf form, Peter committed numerous terrible acts, including eating the beating hearts of some of his victims and murdering his own son. In all, he killed more than a dozen people, as well as a number of sheep, goats, and lambs. Incredibly, the story of Peter Stubbe's outrageous behavior ends with his capture while in the process of transforming from a wolf to a man.

After being tortured, Peter confessed to the horrific deeds. His crimes were so shocking that instead of being burned at the stake, he was strapped to a wheel, tortured, and beheaded. His body was then burned.

To warn others against committing any such crimes, the torture wheel was attached to a pole and erected in the town. Atop the wheel was a figure of a wolf . . . and Peter's severed head!

Some people say that Peter Stubbe was charged with his crimes for political reasons—that he was not, in fact, guilty. Some believe he—like others convicted in werewolf trials—was a real-life serial killer, a deeply disturbed individual who believed he turned into a wolf before his murderous rampages. The truth is unknown.

What's clear is that the fear of werewolves and a belief in the supernatural were still widespread and powerful more than three thousand years after the *Epic of Gilgamesh*. But as the Renaissance—an era of new ideas and inventions—took hold across Europe, scientists began offering their own explanations for werewolf phenomena.

The Beast of Gévaudan

From 1764 to 1767, the Gévaudan region of southern France was terrorized by an unknown beast. Witnesses said the animal was "like a wolf, yet not a wolf"—it was larger, with reddish gray hair, a long tail, and a black stripe on its back. More than one hundred people were killed, and some wondered if multiple beasts were responsible.

Not everyone who was attacked died. One young woman pierced the beast's chest with a spear. Another time, a group of eight children fought the monster off with sticks. Stories about the Beast of Gévaudan appeared in newspapers as far away as North America! Could the beast be a werewolf?

King Louis XV sent royal hunters to Gévaudan, and soon, a large wolf was shot. The attacks stopped . . . for a while. Later, a second large wolf was killed. It matched the unusual description given by witnesses and supposedly had human remains inside its stomach.

CHAPTER 3
Lycanthropy

The concept of lycanthropy—the belief that one is a wolf or can transform into a wolf—has been around since ancient times. In ancient Greece, lycanthropes (people with lycanthropy) were said to suffer from dryness of the eyes and tongue and melancholy, which is a deep sadness. They roamed the outdoors at night, often through graveyards, howling like wolves. But they were not considered a danger to themselves or others.

During this time, the lines between medicine and magic blurred together. Over the centuries, though, science became less intertwined with superstition, and ideas on lycanthropy began to change.

By the time of the werewolf trials, people had begun to think of lycanthropy as a type of mental illness. Lycanthropes were more often considered madmen and madwomen than they were sorcerers or shape-shifting werewolves.

Physicians were sometimes called to testify at werewolf trials. Over time, their opinions became more widely trusted than some religious opinions. One man wrote that "the transformations, which these witch-mongers do so rave and rage upon, is . . . a disease . . . whereby many suppose themselves to be wolves."

Even if werewolves were not actually wolves, lycanthropes could still be dangerous.

In 1603, near Bordeaux, France, thirteen-year-old Jean Grenier became possibly the youngest person convicted in a werewolf trial. One spring day, two young shepherd girls came upon Jean sitting on a log. He had large canine teeth, black pointed nails, and bright, sunken, fierce eyes. Jean said he looked that way because he sometimes wore a wolf skin.

He told the girls that three nights a week, he donned his wolf pelt and turned into a wolf—and raided the countryside with nine other werewolves. Jean said he'd killed and eaten dogs, but that girls' blood tasted better. "If the sun were to set," he told them, "I would soon fall on one of you and make a meal of you!" Jean broke into wild laughter, and the girls ran away, terrified.

A number of other girls in the area had recently gone missing, and Jean was soon arrested and questioned. He admitted to attacking and killing some of the children. He also claimed that when he was ten or eleven, he'd sold his soul to the devil and was given an ointment and a wolf skin that transformed him into a wolf.

The court ruled that Jean Grenier suffered from "mere hallucination" and a "disorganized brain of the insane." Jean was sentenced to life imprisonment in a monastery, where monks would instruct him in the ways of Christianity and service to God.

Jean never recovered from his delusions. He ran around the monastery on all fours and ate raw meat. Over time, he became withdrawn, rarely spoke, and avoided eye contact. His physical condition worsened, and he eventually died when he was just twenty years old.

Another famous case of similar mental illness occurred in northern Italy in 1541, when a peasant viciously attacked a group of farmers in their fields. He slashed at them with his teeth, killing several.

When the killer was captured, he claimed that he was a wolf, but "whereas wolves are hairy outside," he told them, "my fur grows within my body." His captors made cuts into his skin to check for fur underneath, but they found none. It was all in the man's mind.

As the idea that lycanthropy was a mental condition became more widely accepted, werewolf trials finally ended. Werewolves were increasingly regarded as myths and folktales from another time, and people who believed they were werewolves were considered mentally ill.

Society was changing rapidly. The Renaissance had led to the Age of Enlightenment, when new ideas like freedom of religion, and celebration of science and reason, were taking hold across the world. But thanks to the relatively new invention of the printing press, legends and stories of werewolves would continue to spread.

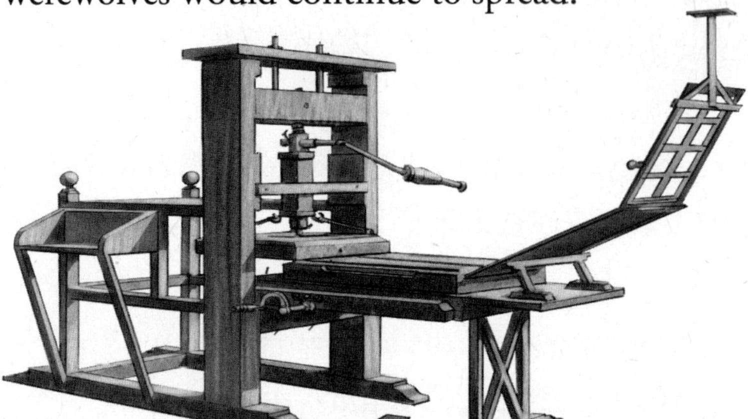

Printing press

CHAPTER 4
Werewolves in Literature

Since the beginning of human history, werewolf stories have been passed down orally (by telling them out loud), from generation to generation. Some of these stories were eventually recorded in books and on scrolls. Copies were

Ovid

painstakingly made by hand, word by word.

After the invention of the movable-type printing press in Europe around 1440, books could be mass-produced and read by many more people. Werewolf tales told by ancient writers like Ovid and Herodotus were suddenly reaching a much bigger audience.

The folktale of "Little Red Riding Hood" was first printed in a book in France in 1697. In the story, a girl called Little Red Riding Hood is stalked by a wolf as she walks through the woods to her sick grandmother's house. The wolf runs ahead, finds the girl's grandmother, and swallows her whole. He then disguises himself as the old woman and waits for the girl. When she arrives, he eats her, too!

Though not a werewolf story, "Little Red Riding Hood" reinforced the idea that wolves were evil and dangerous, and not to be trusted. Today, it is still one of the first stories many children are read.

In 1612, John Webster of England began writing *The Duchess of Malfi*, a play in which the villain, Ferdinand, is a werewolf. The story was heavily inspired by real events, with some passages matching records of werewolf trials word for word.

Writers didn't really create their own werewolf stories until the 1800s. During this time, gothic horror novels—a blend of mystery, horror, and the supernatural—were all the rage. The books were called "gothic" for the architectural style of their creepy settings, which were often large, decaying mansions or creepy castles. Readers couldn't get enough of books like Mary Wollstonecraft Shelley's *Frankenstein* (1818), Edgar Allan Poe's *The Fall of the House of Usher* (1839), and Bram Stoker's *Dracula* (1897).

George W. M. Reynolds was one of England's most popular writers. His 1847 book *Wagner, the Wehr-Wolf* was one of the first to feature a werewolf. When the title character, Wagner, makes a pact with the devil for youth, money, and beauty, he must become a wolf on the final night of every month. Wagner flees to the desert but is unable to escape the evil that haunts him.

George W. M. Reynolds

In 1896, Clemence Housman published her first novel, *The Were-Wolf*. Clemence's brother Laurence created eerie illustrations for the book. The story is set in a small Scandinavian village that is being stalked by a monster. The monster is White Fell, a female werewolf who lures men to their death with her enchanting charm.

While not technically a werewolf story, Robert Louis Stevenson's *The Strange Case of Dr. Jekyll and Mr. Hyde* (1886) contains themes found in werewolf legends. It inspired werewolf movies of the twentieth century and multiple movies of its own.

Dr. Henry Jekyll is an upstanding citizen living in London's West End. The well-respected doctor has a dark side, however: He struggles with violent urges. So, Dr. Jekyll concocts an elixir in his laboratory that, when drunk, transforms him into Edward Hyde, his evil alternate personality. "Man is not truly one but truly two," Jekyll says.

The devious, animalistic Mr. Hyde roams the poorer neighborhoods of London to satisfy his impulses. Dr. Jekyll has no control over Mr. Hyde during these nighttime escapades. At one point, Mr. Hyde tramples an innocent girl.

He even commits murder. "My devil had long been caged," Jekyll says. "He came out roaring."

Over time, Dr. Jekyll realizes he must prevent Hyde from emerging. He stops taking the elixir.

Then one morning, what Jekyll sees in the mirror turns his blood cold. "I had gone to bed Henry Jekyll, I had awakened Edward Hyde." The book ends with Jekyll/Hyde's death. "Evil finally destroyed the balance of my soul."

Robert Louis Stevenson was inspired by a vivid nightmare to write *Jekyll and Hyde*. It took him just three days to complete the first draft.

Perhaps the most famous werewolf novel is by American author Guy Endore. *The Werewolf of Paris* became a #1 *New York Times* bestseller when it published in 1933. Some consider it to be the *Dracula* of werewolf literature. To help control his transformations, the book's main character has to drink his girlfriend's blood.

The Werewolf of Paris might sound more like a vampire story than a typical werewolf tale. During the twentieth century, writers—and then moviemakers—began adding their own twists to traditional werewolf stories. These new takes on ancient legends brought werewolves back into people's imaginations.

They've been lurking there ever since.

Robert Louis Stevenson (1850–1894)

Robert Louis Stevenson was born in Edinburgh, Scotland, and suffered from poor health all his life. At sixteen, he enrolled at the University of Edinburgh, where his outlandish fashion sense earned him the nickname "Velvet Jacket." Robert's father expected him to follow in his footsteps and become a lighthouse engineer, but Robert wanted to write.

While in California in 1880, Robert married Fanny Osbourne, an American writer. They returned to Scotland with Fanny's son, Lloyd. One rainy summer day, twelve-year-old Lloyd was entertaining himself by drawing pictures. Robert joined him. They drew a map of an island that inspired one of history's most famous children's books. Stevenson's *Treasure Island* (1883), featuring the pirate Long John Silver, introduced many concepts people now associate with pirates, like one-legged buccaneers and treasure maps where *X* marks the spot.

Robert and his family moved all around the world in search of a climate that would be better for Robert's health. At forty-four, he died on the Pacific island of Samoa, where Samoans had given him the name Tusitala, or teller of tales.

CHAPTER 5
Starring: The Wolf Man!

Werewolves jumped from page to screen for the first time in 1913 in a silent film called *The Werewolf*. The movie told the story of a Native American woman who turned into a wolf.

Movies did not yet feature sound, and the film was just eighteen minutes long.

In *Wolfblood* (1925), a man is injured in a fight and requires a blood transfusion. But with no human blood available, the doctor uses a wolf's blood instead. Some time later, after a townsperson is found dead, rumors swirl about the wolf-blooded man, who begins to believe he is a monster.

Much of what people know today about werewolf mythology is because of the werewolf movies of the early twentieth century. The very first time it was suggested that a wolf bite could turn someone into a werewolf was in Universal Pictures' *Werewolf of London* (1935).

It wasn't until 1941 in *The Wolf Man*, history's most famous werewolf movie, that the werewolf's transformation became connected to the moon: "Even a man who is pure in heart, and says his prayers by night, may become a wolf when the wolfbane blooms and the autumn moon is bright." (The first time the *full* moon caused the werewolf transformation was in the 1943 sequel, *Frankenstein Meets the Wolf*

Man.) Before these two movies, the moon had surprisingly nothing to do with werewolf legends.

Actor Lon Chaney Jr. played the parts of Lawrence Talbot, known as Larry, and the Wolf Man. One night, Larry hears a woman crying out in the woods. She is being attacked by a wolf! Larry is bitten, but he beats the wolf to death with a silver cane. This film was also one of the first times that silver was introduced as harmful to werewolves.

The next morning, a man's body—a visiting fortune teller—is found where Larry killed the wolf. Larry is told the man was a werewolf who'd transformed back into his human form after he died. The fortune teller's mother tells Larry: "Whoever is bitten by a werewolf and lives . . . becomes a werewolf himself."

The following night, Larry transforms into the Wolf Man and murders a gravedigger. The next morning, Larry awakens in his room in his human form. He has no memory of what happened the night before, but when he sees the muddy paw prints leading to his bed, he understands the terrible truth.

For the rest of the movie, Larry wrestles with his guilt and begs the people around him to lock him up and to stay away from him. In the end, he is killed by the same silver cane he used to kill the fortune-teller werewolf at the beginning of the movie.

Universal released *The Wolf Man* on December 9, 1941, two days after the Japanese attack on Pearl Harbor brought the United States into World War II. The war had already been raging overseas for two years.

During wartime, the line between good and evil can become less clear. If a soldier defending their homeland kills a soldier from an invading army, does that make them evil?

Audiences connected with *The Wolf Man*'s themes of good against evil, and guilt over one's actions during difficult times.

They also thought the monster looked pretty cool!

It took makeup artist Jack Pierce six hours to turn Lon Chaney into the Wolf Man. (It then took up to three hours to *remove* the makeup!)

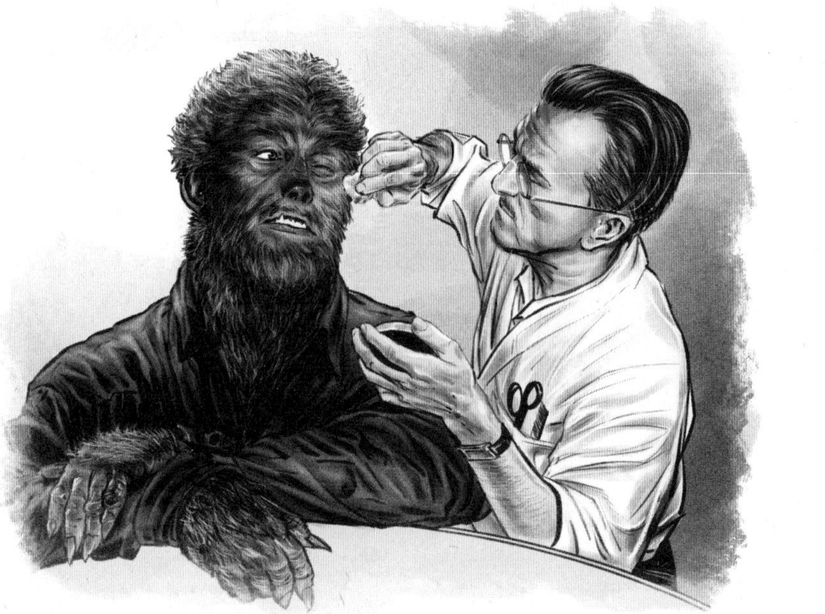

In a "typical" werewolf transformation, a person turns from a human into a wolf. The Wolf Man was a frightening combination of both. The iconic movie monster had long nails and canine teeth and was covered in fur but stood upright like a man. (Jack Pierce had also worked on 1935's *Werewolf of London*, but the actor who played that werewolf refused to sit for such a long time for makeup!)

It took Oscar-winning makeup artist Rick Baker just as long to create the monster in 1981's *An American Werewolf in London*. And the transformation scene alone took six days to film!

In the movie, two American college students named David and Jack are backpacking through the foggy English countryside. At a pub, the young men are warned by local men to stick to the road on their journey.

Later, when the Americans veer off the path, they are attacked by an enormous wolflike creature. Jack is killed. The local men arrive to shoot the monster dead before it can kill David. Just as David passes out, he sees that the wolf has become a naked man.

Weeks later, David wakes up in a hospital in London. Throughout the movie, he has terrible nightmares that feel frighteningly real. He is visited by his dead friend Jack, who tells him they were both attacked by a werewolf, and at the next full moon, David will become one himself. Sure enough, Jack is telling the truth, and David transforms. He tears through the city's streets and subway tunnels, now as an American werewolf in London.

The 1941 *Wolf Man* film had ushered in a new era of werewolf legends, inspiring countless movies, books, and short stories. Many new tales became new werewolf movies. Superstar authors Stephen King and R. L. Stine—who have each sold hundreds of millions of books over their careers—each wrote werewolf stories that were turned into movies.

Silver Bullet (1985) was based on Stephen King's novella *Cycle of the Werewolf*. (A novella

Stephen King

R. L. Stine

is a short novel.) The movie is set in a small Maine town where a series of gruesome unsolved murders has taken place. Actor Corey Haim plays Marty, a boy who uses a wheelchair, and Gary Busey stars as Marty's uncle Red. On the Fourth of July, Uncle Red surprises Marty with a souped-up wheelchair-motorcycle he nicknames the Silver Bullet. Marty sneaks out later to take the Silver Bullet for a spin and set off fireworks by a lake . . . where he encounters a giant werewolf.

Marty shoots a firework into the monster's eye and escapes, but later, the wolf comes looking for Marty and his family.

Marty's Silver Bullet

R. L. Stine, creator of the Goosebumps series for young readers, published *The Werewolf of Fever Swamp* in 1993. It tells the story of twelve-year-old Grady Tucker, who moves with his family from Vermont to Fever Swamp, Florida.

Grady befriends a local boy named Will Blake, who is later revealed to be a werewolf. The book was adapted into a movie that aired on television in 1996. Will Blake's werewolf also appears in the 2015 *Goosebumps* movie.

Werewolves appear in many other popular books, movies, and shows for kids and young adults. *Teen Wolf* (1985) was a comedy starring Michael J. Fox as Scott Howard, a teenager from a family of werewolves. Unlike in other werewolf movies, Scott can control his actions when in his wolf form—though his father warns him not to lose his temper! Scott becomes the hero of his

Michael J. Fox

school's basketball team but soon comes to rely on the wolf's powers to succeed. *Teen Wolf* inspired a popular teen-drama TV series of the same name that ran from 2011 to 2017.

Actor Seth Green plays another teen wolf, Oz, in the television series *Buffy the Vampire Slayer*, which aired from 1997 to 2003. For the three nights around the full moon, Oz transforms into a wolf. When his friends find out, they decide to help Oz by locking him in a cage and keeping watch until the full moon wanes.

The animated movie *Hotel Transylvania* (2012) features the character Wayne Werewolf, a data processor who hates his job. As the father of *dozens* of wolf pups, Wayne doesn't get much sleep and is always exhausted. The highlight of Wayne's year is when he and his wife, Wanda Werewolf, take their annual family vacation to Hotel Transylvania.

The Harry Potter series features Professor Remus Lupin, a popular teacher at Hogwarts School of Witchcraft and Wizardry. But Lupin harbors a secret: Every full moon, he becomes a wolf. However, he uses a potion to control his animal side: "As long as I take it in the week preceding the full moon, I keep my mind when I transform. . . . I am able to curl up in my office, a harmless wolf, and wait for the moon to wane again."

The Twilight Saga features Jacob Black, a boy who first turns into a wolf at age sixteen. His tribe, the Quileute, has this transformative power. Jacob competes with a vampire named Edward Cullen for the love of a girl named Bella Swan. Wolves and vampires in Twilight are bitter rivals, as they are in many other modern stories.

A crew films *Eclipse*, the third film of the Twilight Saga

Both the Harry Potter and Twilight series of books were adapted into wildly successful movie franchises. Over the decades, many werewolf movies spun off multiple sequels and remakes.

Shape-Shifters

It is revealed later in the Twilight series that Jacob is not a true werewolf but a shape-shifter. True werewolves—known as the Children of the Moon in the Twilight books—required the full moon to transform, and they became wild and uncontrolled in their wolf form. Jacob and his people inherited their shape-shifting abilities from their ancestors, unlike the Children of the Moon, who needed to be infected by another werewolf. And they are in full control of their actions while in their wolf form.

Shape-shifters—beings that can change at will into another type of being—have appeared in legends for as long as werewolves. A werewolf is a type of shape-shifter, but there are many others, such as the Ethiopian werehyena, also known as *bouda*, meaning "evil eye." Werehyenas can be human-born or hyenas disguised as humans. Like wolves in Europe and the Americas, hyenas are top predators in Africa and have competed with humans since the beginning of history. In Central America, the ancient Olmecs believed in werejaguars. Shape-shifters can also be animals that shift into human form. The fabled selkie of Irish mythology are seals that remove their skins to become human.

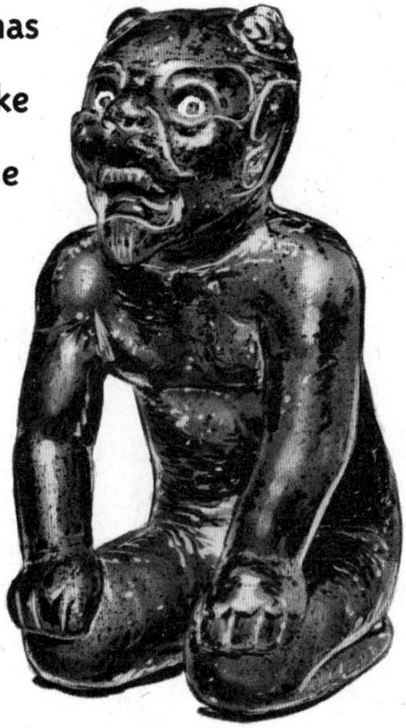

Werejaguar statue

The Wolf Man was remade in 2010, with Benicio del Toro in the role of Lawrence Talbot and Anthony Hopkins as his father, Sir John Talbot. The 2025 *Wolf Man* film was inspired by the original. Perhaps to honor the movie's place in history, the new version of the monster was created without any computer-generated elements—only makeup and practical effects were used.

Werewolves are even popular toys. In 2010, Mattel released their line of Monster High fashion dolls. Clawdeen Wolf, a teenage werewolf, was among the first characters. She attends Monster High in the fictional town of New Salem with children of other famous monsters. Clawdeen acts a little "freaky" around the full moon—or under a spotlight—and appears in multiple Monster High cartoons, TV specials, and books.

Werewolves are everywhere now. On the big screen, on our tablets, in our books, and in our video games. But are they still . . . *out there*?

CHAPTER 6
United States of Werewolves

While much of popular werewolf mythology originated in Europe, Native Americans have their own werewolf and supernatural legends. The Navajo skin-walkers are thought to be shape-shifters with glowing eyes who put hexes on people and robbed graves. The wendigos were cannibals possessed by demons that made them crave human flesh. When Europeans colonized the Americas, they brought their own superstitions with them. Over time, the different folklores influenced one another.

Even in the modern era, there have been many sightings of strange creatures resembling werewolves in the United States.

In the Wisconsin countryside in 1936, a night watchman named Mark Shackleman spotted a shadow across a field while on his shift. It was a large figure—bigger than a dog or a wolf—hunched over on all fours. It was digging at a Native American burial mound.

The creature saw Shackleman and stood upright. It was more than six feet tall and covered in long hair. Its face was doglike, its body humanoid. It growled before running off into the forest.

The next night, Shackleman saw the creature again. This time, when the beast growled, the watchman believed it sounded half-human. Again, the creature ran off, and Shackleman never saw it again.

People believe these were the first sightings of what came to be known as the Beast of Bray Road. It is named for the road where it was later spotted, eating roadkill, in 1989.

Encounters with the Beast of Bray Road continued into the late 1990s. There was even a reported sighting in 2020. Witnesses described the beast as five to seven feet tall with glowing eyes. It stood on two legs but ran on four. One woman claimed she hit the Beast with her car.

Beast of Bray Road

When she stopped to see if the animal was injured, it charged at her. She made it back into the car in time and sped off.

Sightings of a similar creature known as the Dogman have been reported throughout rural Texas, even to this day.

Witnesses say the Dogman, like the Beast of Bray Road, has a dog- or wolflike face with glowing eyes and stands on two legs. However, Dogman is reportedly larger—anywhere from seven to eleven feet in height! It moves with frightening speed and is sometimes said to appear as if out of nowhere, like a supernatural force.

Could these be sightings of real werewolves?

There is no hard evidence—photos, video, footprints—to indicate that they are. And many theories have been offered to explain these encounters. Many believe that it could have been a bear with mange, a skin condition that could alter the animal's physical appearance enough to confuse witnesses.

A bear with mange

During the werewolf trials, people testified in court that they had seen werewolves in the flesh. Witnessed their magical transformations. Been the victims of their vicious attacks. Were they wrong? Had they actually seen what they thought they saw?

For the people who claim to have encountered the Dogman or the Beast of Bray Road, what they saw and experienced was real to them. Whether or not their stories are believed doesn't change that.

CHAPTER 7
Are Werewolves Real?

If humans have believed in werewolves for thousands of years, is it possible that werewolves are real? If werewolves *don't* exist, how could we have been wrong for so long?

There are some possible scientific explanations for werewolf phenomena.

Hypertrichosis is an extremely rare genetic disorder that causes excessive hair growth all over the face and body. In the late 1880s, a sixteen-year-old boy with hypertrichosis named Fedor Jeftichew joined P. T. Barnum's circus as a sideshow act. He was known as "Jo-Jo the Dog-Faced Boy."

Fedor Jeftichew

Today we understand that it was cruel and unkind that Fedor was treated as an exhibit and put on display. He was as human as anyone else. But a person with hypertrichosis in fifteenth-century Europe might have suffered a worse, or even deadlier, fate.

Rabies is another possible explanation for werewolfish behavior. It is an extremely dangerous disease carried by animals—like wolves and dogs—and can be transmitted with a bite or a scratch. Rabid animals act aggressively and will attack people for no reason.

A person infected with rabies might experience hallucinations—seeing things that aren't there and believing things that aren't true. These symptoms mirror the werewolf myths very closely.

Could the moon play a role in werewolf phenomena?

Some studies have shown that crime increases under a full moon, and people have long believed the full moon can cause violent behavior. In fact, the words *lunacy* and *lunatic* come from *Luna*, the Roman goddess of the moon. And a person on trial for murder in eighteenth-century England could even ask for a lighter sentence if the crime happened under a full moon. Today, though, some people believe that an increase in crime during the full moon is simply due to the fact that those nights are brighter—which makes it easier for criminals to see.

As our understanding of the world around us has evolved over time, so too has our belief in werewolves.

Early in our history, we looked to wolves for inspiration and courage. We wore their skins and pretended to be them, drew strength from their animal spirit, feared and respected them. To become a wolf was to become one with one of nature's most formidable predators.

Our perception of wolves changed when some religious and political people began equating them with the forces of evil. Werewolves and dark magic became ways to explain how certain people could commit shocking and violent acts. At a time when humanity was shifting from a rural existence to an urban one, werewolves represented all that was wicked in the uncivilized wilderness.

As Christianity's influence decreased and science began to take hold, werewolfism was considered to be the product of the human mind. Mental illness is what caused a person to believe they became a wolf, not an enchanted belt or a pact with the devil.

In modern times, the werewolf has come to symbolize the duality of human nature: our human side and our animal side. Our civilized side and our wild side. Even if humans can't physically shape-shift into wolves, might we all have a little werewolf within us?

As Sir John Talbot said in the original *Wolf Man*: "Good, bad, right, wrong, are many-sided, complex things. We try to see every side, but the more we see, the less sure we are."

Timeline of Werewolves

c. 2000 BCE	Ancient Babylonian text *Epic of Gilgamesh* features story of the goddess Ishtar turning a suitor into a wolf
c. 700 BCE	Story of Zeus turning King Lycaon into a wolf appears in the first written origin story of Greek mythology
c. 64 CE	Story of Niceros, a servant whose traveling companion transforms into a wolf, appears in Roman writer Petronius's *Satyricon*
c. 1160–1175	Marie de France writes the story *Bisclavret* about a werewolf nobleman who becomes trapped in his wolf body by his wife
1428	Werewolf trials begin in Europe
1603	Jean Grenier becomes the youngest defendant in a werewolf trial; his werewolfism is ruled a mental illness
1933	Guy Endore's *The Werewolf of Paris* becomes a #1 *New York Times* bestseller
1941	Universal Pictures releases *The Wolf Man*
1982	*An American Werewolf in London* wins the first Oscar for makeup
1993	R. L. Stine's *The Werewolf of Fever Swamp* is published
2010	Mattel releases Monster High fashion dolls, including Clawdeen Wolf
2025	*Wolf Man*, Universal's reboot of the horror classic, hits movie theaters

Timeline of the World

c. 2500 BCE	A circle of large stones is erected at Stonehenge
753 BCE	The city of Rome is founded
710 BCE	The first known lock and key is fitted at a palace in Assyria (modern-day Iraq)
31 CE	Jesus of Nazareth is crucified outside Jerusalem
43	The Roman army invades Britain
c. 1170	*The Mystery of Adam*, the first known mystery play, is performed in France
1429	Joan of Arc, guided by the voices of the saints, leads French military forces against the English in the liberation of Orléans
1607	Jamestown, the first British settlement in America, is established in Virginia
1692–93	The Salem witch trials are held in Massachusetts Bay Colony
1933	Adolf Hitler and the Nazi Party rise to power in Germany
1981	Andrew Lloyd Webber's musical *Cats* opens in London
2010	A massive 7.0-magnitude earthquake rocks Haiti, killing more than two hundred thousand
2025	The Los Angeles area suffers its worst wildfires in history

Bibliography

Baring-Gould, Sabine. ***The Book of Werewolves***. London: Smith, Elder & Co., 1865.

de Blécourt, Willem, ed. ***Werewolf Histories*** (Palgrave Historical Studies in Witchcraft and Magic series). Basingstoke, England, and New York: Palgrave Macmillan, 2015.

Stebbins, Maegan A. ***The Werewolf: Past and Future: Lycanthropy's Lost History & Modern Devolution***. Published by the author, 2021.

Summers, Montague. ***The Werewolf in Lore and Legend***. Mineola, NY: Dover Publications, 2003.